Foreword

For the past 10 years I have been living in a love-hate relationship with one of the most complex animals on the planet: a housecat.

It has been a tumultuous association. One moment he's a loving, purring bundle of fur snuggling into my lap. The next, a hissing, spitting yowling ball of fury, eager to inflict injury for real or imagined wrongs.

People who are owned by cats know that they have a untamed animal living in their home. They may be the size of a bunny rabbit, but cats have the heart and fierce independence of a lion.

At the same time, they can be affectionate and loyal creatures and wonderful, easy to maintain companions.

During my decade with my cat, Spook, (named because of his eerie glowing sometimes blazing yellow, sometimes frigid green eyes making him look like a satanic creature out of a Stephen King novel) we have had many adventures together.

I made him a regular subject in my weekly humor columns at The Blade and he has enjoyed a certain celebrity over the years. In fact, nobody ever asks how I am, they always inquire, "So, how's Spook doing?"

After often being asked why I never made those columns into a book, I decided to do just that. Here are a group of my favorite columns about Spook, whom I would like to thank sincerely. Without him, this book would not have been possible.

Tom Ensign,
Toledo Ohio,
January, 2000

*To anyone who
has ever been owned by a cat.*

Table of Contents

Chapter 1
Getting Acquainted

I have rug burns on my body.

I got them from chasing my cat in my underwear.

No, no, the cat wasn't wearing my underwear; that would be sick.

But, then, I don't suppose any of this sounds like the epitome of mental health.

Perhaps I should explain.

Why was I chasing the cat in my unmentionables? Well, it was 5 a.m. and I was driven by blind rage. I really didn't want to hurt him. I wanted to kill him.

Of course, that's impossible. Did you ever try to catch a cat that's gleefully careening around the room, ripping out plugs, knocking over lamps, and tearing the curtains?

The Humane Society need not worry. The Spook is in no danger.

He's not only faster and more agile than me, but what really hurts is that he seems to be a good deal smarter.

One time, while under the influence of a stupid attack, I got to feeling lonely. I couldn't think of any women — or men for that matter — with whom I wanted to share housekeeping. (Actually, there is a woman with whom I would be delighted to share my bed and board, but Demi Moore lacks a mutual interest.)

So, why not a pet?

I like dogs, but weird working hours and travel make a dog impractical.

How about a cat?

Well, I thought, why not? They're independent and don't need much attention. Plus, even an indoor cat can do nicely if left alone for a couple of days as long as there's plenty of food and water and a clean sand box.

A former friend suggested the Humane Society — "Plenty of free cats there," he said.

Hah.

While wandering around the facility's cat room (no, it's not called a cat house) I felt a gentle tug on my shoulder. A solid black feline somewhere between kitten and cat had tentatively reached out to get my attention.

"Yo, Tom! I'm the one you want," he seemed to say, giving me the full blast of glowing yellow eyes. He had an almost mesmerizing effect. It was, well, spooky. Immediately he became The Spook.

I was hooked. I was ready to pack him up and gallop off.

But you don't just find a cat and walk out. Oh, no. First you have to fill out adoption papers. Then you talk to a counselor who apparently decides whether or not you will be a fit parent. Then, if you live in an apartment, they squeal on you.

My apartment complex allows pets, but you have to pay a $100 deposit and an extra $10 a month. Since the cat was going to stay forever indoors, I wasn't going to say anything about our new addition. That idea was shattered when the Humane Society worker called the manager to make sure I was truthful about animals being allowed.

I also paid $22 for the lousy cat (his stock was falling fast) as well as a $10 deposit that would be returned as soon as he was neutered. So far, I hadn't even walked out of the place and I had already shelled out $132 for my free cat.

And I was facing more expenses.

When I got Spook home, I found to my chagrin that he liked to play Tarzan, swinging wildly from the drapes to the tablecloth. Declawing became the first order of business.

Neutering didn't seem like a bad idea, either. For years people have told me to neuter even an indoor cat because it "sprays." I never knew what that meant, exactly, until one day at the zoo when the lion, for no reason other than orneriness, backed up against the bars and let loose with a stream that doused a pack of visiting Girl Scouts.

Although not expecting a troop of scouts in my apartment (worse luck), I thought it best to get both claws and manhood lopped off at the same time. There went another $80, and Spook still had his back claws intact.

The folks at the vets said that was because if he ever got outside, he could defend himself.

What they didn't say was that inside, it would help in his quest to be a one-cat wrecking crew.

Shortly after we settled in together, I discovered that I had an animal that had sprung from the loins of Satan.

The drapes are but shredded strands of dismal string. There is no more tablecloth ... nor much of a table for that matter. Nothing is safe. He opens kitchen cabinets and hurls everything to the floor so he can destroy it later at his leisure.

At first I tried to reason with him. After all, he came from the mean streets and perhaps just needed some understanding and love.

What he needs is a solid clout. I carry assorted gouges and scratch marks all over my body from when he uses me as a launching pad or when we play and he tries to see how many strips he can slice my hand into.

But the worst is the caterwauling

I don't let him sleep with me because he usually wakes up between 3 and 5 a.m., feeling frisky and gnawing at my feet.

When he gets locked out of the bedroom, he screams about it. This usually elicits a frustrated curse from me and I charge from the bed, fling open the door, and shout idle threats.

"SHADDUP YOU DIRTY LITTLE HUN!" I bellow. "THAT'S IT. TOMORROW YOU'RE GOING BACK TO JAIL! I MEAN IT!"

Eyes bright with anticipation, he cagily scampers far enough away to lure me from the door, then dashes into bedroom and ducks under the sanctity of the bed.

I am close to tears.

The other night, I refused to be baited. I ignored his screeching and he eventually stopped. Complimenting myself, I began to doze off when I heard a crash.

The Spook had knocked the lamp off the living room end table. He was nowhere to be seen. Well, it might have been an accident.

I again snuggled beneath the covers only to bolt upright when the same crash occurred. That did it. In a blind rage, I flew from the room, waving a bamboo back scratcher threateningly. I was going to have my vengeance.

I have no idea what my poor upstairs neighbor must have thought about the hysterical curses followed by thuds and slamming as I knocked over chairs and hurled away furniture in a mad attack.

Spook loved it. He scampered behind the furniture, gaily ripping out wires and knocking glass items from shelves. I don't know how long this went on before we both spotted something at the same time. I had left the bedroom door open!

We both spurted for the door and I made one last valiant flying leap to block him. I left most of my skin on the floor and he left me clutching a few strands of black fur. All I could see were those gleaming eyes mocking me from beneath the bed.

I'm a beaten man. I can't help but foster a grudging respect for anything that can thrash me so totally. Besides, there are some good points. When he's not destroying something, he'll fetch paper balls I crumple up and throw at a spittoon across the room.

And, while he might be a menace, he certainly isn't dull.

I'm beginning to love hating him.

Chapter 2
Joy of Living Together

Living alone is wonderful — you don't have to share anything with anyone.

Living alone is terrible — you don't have anyone to share things with, but you can easily learn to live with that.

I've been batching it for some time now and lean toward the notion that going the solo route isn't really so bad. In fact, it can be great fun. It's kind of like being Peter Pan. You don't have to grow up.

You don't have to do anything you don't want to do any time you don't want to do it.

If you want to eat a peanut butter and carrot sandwich for dinner, nobody cares. If you want to leave your underwear on the floor, so be it. You don't have to vacuum, sweep, mop, dust, disinfect, squeegie, or pick up newspapers unless you want to.

Now, I ask you, is this gracious living or what?

There are those who differ with me, and I hear from them every now and then.

"Tom," they tell me, looking around the shambles of my apartment in head-shaking pity. "You *really* need to get a wife."

I can't for the life of me think why.

"Look," I counter, "I've got an overweight cat that sleeps all day, talks too much, and stays out all night. Why in the hell would I need a wife?"

I got my cat, The Spookmeister, to act as sort of a surrogate wife (a platonic relationship, I assure you). This was not one of my better ideas. Spook is the cat from hell.

There is no comfort or affection here, just constant nagging, demands, gripes, and sheer nastiness.

I don't know why we stay together. I guess it's because I'm a little afraid of him. One friend described him as a cross between a panther and a grizzly bear.

We have an understanding. I feed him and he lets me live.

Spook is also what gives me my greatest feeling of terror about living alone. Death.

Oh, I'm not afraid of him dying. A quick service and a brown paper bag funeral in the dumpster. No problem.

No, the terror is in *my* death. Not the death itself, but the "afterdeath."

I'm worried my corpse will disappear.

If I were to succumb to a goiter attack or something on, say, a Friday evening, it would probably be days before anyone would actually investigate to see what happened to me.

My daughter calls me about once a week, but if I'm not home, she wouldn't be overly concerned, at least not for several days.

If I didn't show for work on Monday, the people at The Blade would wonder. But after calling and not receiving an answer they might presume that I had taken a day off or a few days' vacation that got lost in the computer.

So in theory, I could be long dead and nobody would know.

Nobody...except the cat.

Spook would know. And when his food ran out, he'd be getting hungry. I can picture him creeping up and sniffing my dead toe, perhaps taking a quick nip to see if I'll come leaping out of bed and hit him over the head with a back scratcher like I usually do.

But no, I would be still. And his confidence would grow along with his hunger.

Then, a week or so later when everyone decides something is definitely amiss, I can picture the authorities breaking into the apartment and finding no trace of me -- nothing except for a few gray curly hairs the 250-pound cat is flossing with.

A few months later, I'll be the lead story on *Unsolved Mysteries*.

So, folks, if you don't hear from me for a day or two break down the apartment door, will you? I will be eternally grateful.

Oh, and shoot the cat.

Chapter 3
Tis the season

I can sympathize with Charlie Brown.

You know, he's that "Peanuts" character who every year gets suckered in by Lucy when she tells him to kick the football while she holds it. She then yanks it away just as Charlie swings his foot, and he winds up flat on his back.

You're not alone, Charlie. I have the same problem...sort of. Instead of Lucy and a football, I have Spook and a Christmas tree.

Spook, my nasty cat with terrorist tendencies, is fascinated with my puny Christmas tree and fiercely dedicated to its destruction.

It was our third Christmas together, and I had hoped that he might have mellowed.

A friend gave me this three-foot-tall artificial tree three years ago. The first year, I bought some lights, bulbs, garland, the works.

The Spook's eyes glistened with unholy glee as I proudly dressed the tree. It took me a couple of hours and I left the room for two minutes. During that time he totally denuded the thing. Ornaments were shattered and strewn across the room. Garlands were unraveled and hung sloppily from various pieces of furniture. The string of lights was chewed completely through, and Spook, tinsel dangling crazily from his ears, was busily pulling the tree across the living room.

I was, justifiably I think, outraged. Raining curses upon his family, I took up chase with a broom, but he easily dodged the blows and hid behind the couch.

That was the end of year one. Last year I figured he was older and wiser. After all, he was just a kid, a crazy kid, the first season. he didn't destroy much of anything during the rest of the year and I thought maybe, just maybe ...

I took the tree out of the box and let it stand in the corner for a day or two. After a couple of initial curious sniffs, he walked away.

Ahhh. I ran out and bought new lights, ornaments, tinsel, etc. He seemed only mildly interested.

Then, in the middle of the night, I heard a tremendous crash (I had put the tree atop the desk). I sprang from my bed to see what was the matter. And what to my wondering eyes did appear but a demolished old tree and a cat with a sneer.

I was close to tears. He had practically promised me he wouldn't murder the tree, but he did anyway.

This year I was determined to forget about the tree. But last Sunday I got bitten by the Christmas-spirit bug again. Spook looked so peaceful, I decided to give it another try.

I pried the tree out of the box, and he seemed totally disinterested. He didn't even bother to sniff. Great. Once again I purchased lights and other neat tree-trimming stuff, but I did learn one lesson. None of the ornaments was made of glass.

I trimmed the tree very slowly and very carefully with a wary eye on Spook. After each step I left him alone in the room with the tree. I then sneaked a peek and was delighted to note that he was busy preening himself and seemed to take no notice whatsoever of the tree.

He did blink a couple of times when I turned the lights on but quickly changed the subject and became extremely intent on the television. The tree? Hah. He wasn't even aware it existed.

After going to bed I waited an hour, and then spurted into the living room and snapped on the light, figuring to catch him in some mischief. I stared in amazement. He was sleeping ... under the tree! Well, that convinced me. All was calm, all was bright. I went to bed fully confident that Spook had finally accepted the tree.

Of course, Monday morning the poor tree was hanging upside down from the desk. The pretty blinking star was crumpled on the floor, and the ornaments and tinsel lie in grotesque lumps on the twisted branches — those that remained connected to the tree.

And so you know what I did? I said the hell with it. If you can't lick 'em, join 'em. So that's where the tree is staying, right where it is. It looks a little strange, I admit, but there's only Spook and me to see it anyway. And there's one big advantage — he can't knock it down again.

Eat your heart out, Charlie Brown.

Chapter 4
Tain't The Season

I have made many pathetic attempts to put up a Christmas tree despite so many problems in the past. As Spook grew older I thought that he surely had gotten all that silliness out of his system. So, once again, I bought a string of lights, some silk bulbs, glittering garland, and an angel with seven bulbs.

It was a beautiful sight. The spirit fairly bubbled through my veins. Spook took an intense interest in the tree trimming but kept a respectful distance. However, there was a malevolent gleam in his eyes as he studied the tree that was perched on the desk.

It was about 20 seconds after I left the room when I heard the crash. He must have hit it at about 90 mph because the tree landed half way across the room and he was busily batting the bulbs off.

Then there was that time when I was sharing a house with a friend and she began to make noises about a Christmas tree. I tried to discourage her, telling her about the lousy history that existed between The Spook and a tree.

She wasn't easily discouraged. In fact, she reasoned that if we got a live, large, and heavy tree, he wouldn't be able to knock it down.

I felt there was only one tree with such a power, and the White House already had it.

Still, a big tree might be a more formidable foe for the cat, but I told her that other precautions were necessary if this was to work at all.

It was extremely important that nothing even remotely breakable be used in the trimming of the tree. Glass ornaments were definitely out. It wasn't that I was worried the cat might hurt himself; it was that broken glass around a tree had an uncanny way of finding a way into bare human feet.

Unbreakable decorations were at a minimum, but we rummaged around the house and found some things that would serve as woefully inadequate albeit fascinating garnishments.

She found an old string of pearls and wrapped them around the top.

A few small hair ribbons were employed as ornaments, and finally we had the finished product.

It wasn't the worst tree I've ever seen. No, the worst was one I put up more than 25 years ago, decorated completely with empty beer cans. It wasn't very pretty, but more than half the fun came in preparing ornaments.

And it's pretty hard to damage a beer can.

I wanted to throw a few of those icicle things at our tree. I've always wanted to do that, but I have never known a woman who will let you do that. Every female from my mother to my ex-wife insisted that you don't throw, you drape them artistically from the branches. It may be prettier, but not nearly as much fun.

This lady had a different reason for saying no. She had read somewhere that if cats were to eat that stuff it might make them ill.

"Yeah, so what's your point?" I asked.

OK, no icicles. The tree was up and finished. We looked at the cat who had been watching the whole procedure with intense interest. Spooky approached with caution, then tentatively batted one of the ribbons from the tree — he was an old hand at this.

After pretty much denuding the tree, though, Spooky was hard pressed to create any real damage. Perhaps he had met his match.

At least I thought so until late that night. First came the tell-tale crash, then she asked, "What was that?"

"Spook knocked over the tree," I sighed as he sauntered into our room, the epitome of innocence. He practically whistled as he ambled across the floor, totally unaware that anything was amiss.

"How do you know it was him?" she asked.

"Well, it doesn't take a genius, based on his past performances ... and how many male cats do you know who wear a string of pearls?"

Christmas. Bah. Humcat.

16

Chapter 5
Cats Are Known to Commit Suicide

Do cats commit suicide?

This may seem a silly question, but it's a subject I've been pondering lately. (As you can see, my mind is cluttered with monumental thoughts.)

I know many cats have a death wish — at least mine certainly seems to, but suicide?

A couple of recent incidents have made me wonder.

I first heard of caticide on a popular 1940s radio show called *The Bickersons*. It starred Don Ameche and Frances Langford as John and Blanche Bickerson, a *Honeymooners*-type couple who constantly sparred with one another in a hilarious fashion.

I'd like it known here that I am far too young to remember *The Bickersons* personally. I have some tapes of the old shows. Really.

One particular skit comes to mind in which Blanche accuses John of killing their feline.

"I didn't kill Nature Boy," John sighs. "He committed suicide, Blanche. Cats have been known to commit suicide."

"Maybe so," she fires back. "but they don't hang themselves."

Of course, the idea seems ridiculous, but now I have second thoughts.

One of the things that made me wonder was when a woman at work mentioned that her cat had somehow gotten its head stuck in a glass jar and couldn't get it out.

When they tried to help it, the cat, who was fully clawed, violently resisted their efforts. It was only when the animal had been weakened by a lack of oxygen that my co-worker was able to subdue the cat and break the jar.

One's first thought is that this incident was an accident, except that few cats are dumb enough to get stuck in a jar. Dogs maybe, but not cats. This animal might have been trying to end it all in a dramatic fashion.

Something even closer to home brought the issue up again.

My cat, Spook, nearly hanged himself and I doubt that, given our volatile relationship, anyone would believe it was a suicide.

The Spook likes to sit in the window and look out at the world he'd like to rule.

When he wants to get up there, he bats me on the leg a few times and runs over to the window so I'll know to raise the blinds.

One day we went through our little ritual and while he was up there, he somehow slipped his head through the cord that raises and lowers the blinds. At least I assume that's what happened. I glanced over just as he was making his leap back to the bed. He stopped in midair and was jerked backward. The cord around his neck twisted a bit, and there he was hanging a few feet from the ground, gesturing and twisting wildly.

Had I not been there, he may well have hanged himself. Against my better judgment, I saved his life for which he showed absolutely no gratitude whatsoever.

In fact, he managed to get a few good scratches in while I was unraveling him.

Was this a freak accident or was he trying to commit suicide, not realizing that I would be intelligent enough to help him out of his dilemma? Or, as I'm sure some vile minds out there will suggest, was it an attempted murder? I'm a little defensive here. After all, the list of suspects is limited.

Chapter 6
A Vi$it to the Vet

Sixty-six dollars and 50 cents!

Can you imagine that? That's what it cost me to take the cat to the veterinarian: $66.50. That's a lot of bucks for a cat that I don't like all that much anyway. I like him about $20 worth. . .maybe. But I sure don't like him $66.50 worth, by any stretch of the imagination.

If I remember correctly, it didn't cost that much to get him fixed. I don't think it cost that much to get *me* fixed.

This all came about the other day when Spook was having a slight bowel problem. I figured it was just nervousness caused by a new environment and a change in food. (We moved in with a lady and her cat, and we steal their food.) The lady suggested I take Spook to the vet. I figured it was probably the right thing to do, since he hadn't been to a vet since I got him several years ago. We made an appointment, and the following Saturday I battled Spooky into a cat's traveling box and we were soon in the waiting room.

That's when I discovered that he enjoyed a certain amount of fame.

"Oh," the assistant said when she looked at him and the registration card.

"Is he that cat that wrecks the house?"

I allowed that it was indeed the home wrecker and she seemed duly impressed.

I was told to bring a sample along with me, and you know what that means. In view of his present condition, this was no problem, but collecting it is never a pleasant task.

It was handed over for analysis, and several minutes later the fact was scientifically confirmed.

It was, indeed, cat poop.

"Oh good," I thought. "I was worried that a raccoon or something had been using our litter box illegally."

By the by, it cost some $9.25 to learn this.

The doctor then came in and went about with the examination, poking here, probing there, inserting a thermometer, prying the mouth open, and generally giving the cat a proper vetting.

Spook was quietly outraged. He didn't say anything, but his angry eyes seemed to say: "You got me into this and you're going to pay pal — big time."

Then came the shots. Oddly enough, he didn't even flinch. Of course, with that much padding, he probably didn't feel the needle anyway.

The first inoculation I really don't understand, but it sounded impressive. On the bill it is described as "rhino.calici.panl.pneum." I think it's to protect him from being trampled by a rhinoceros.

Then there was the rabies shot.

I didn't think he needed one since he never goes outside, but the doctor somberly told me that there was a case where a rabid bat got into a house and infected an indoor cat which in turn bit members of the family.

Does that happen with alarming frequency? I wondered. I was pretty sure the house didn't have any bats — rabid or otherwise.

But, at this point, that was another $14 to protect us from rabid bats.

When the doctor got through with his examination he told me Spook was considerably overweight.

I *knew* that. We are both overweight. It's a glandular thing. We've learned to live with this affliction.

I didn't know exactly how *much* overweight until the assistant put him on the scale.

"He weighs 25 pounds," she said, somewhat unbelieving.

Wow. That's a lot of cat.

I was given some pills and, using two hands, picked up the cat carry-all and began to leave.

Then I remembered something.

"I heard that the first time a cat is a patient here, you take its picture," I said. "How come none was taken of the Spookmeister?"

The assistant shrugged and replied, "We don't have a wide-angle lens."

Like I said, that's a lot of cat.

Chapter 7
A Claw For A Claw

A funny thing happened recently in another chapter in the never-ending saga of me and The Spook.

Under the guise of spirited play, he scratches me and often draws blood. I've tried to retaliate, but it is very difficult to scratch a cat with human claws. In fact, the harder I try, the better he likes it.

Anyway, I thought I had extracted a bit of justice the other day when I took him to the vet.

Since we have been changing residences fairly often over the past couple of years, he has had to change doctors. This hasn't been a great problem because he is too mean to get sick. Still, it had been more than a year since he'd seen a vet, so I made an appointment with a new guy, stuffed him into his carrying box (after a bitter fistfight), and we noisily made our way into the office. I say noisily because Spooky doesn't suffer in silence. He hates the traveling box and yowls in outraged protest until he is released.

The howling persisted while I sat there and filled out the forms. I handed them to the clerk and waited while she tapped the information into her computer.

When we got to the see the doctor, he picked Spook up and exclaimed, "Oh, my, he *is* a big one," Spook was weighed and came in at 22 pounds. I frowned.

"Oh, that's not good," I said.

The vet agreed. "He needs to lose some..."

"No, no," I countered. "Last time he weighed 25 pounds. Do you suppose something's wrong?"

The vet sighed and plunged off into another direction.

"Does he seem healthy? Does he have any problems."

"Oh, he's just fine," I replied. "There's just the diarrhea thing."

The vet asked how long.

"About 18 months," I answered.

"And you didn't see this as a problem?"

"Well, it didn't seem to bother him at all — except he walked kind of funny."

The vet launched into a firm lecture on proper dietary habits. You see, it seems The Spook's problem didn't come about until I started adding canned cat food to his usual dry-food diet-about 18 months ago.

"And it never occurred to you that the two might be linked?" the vet asked through clenched teeth.

"Well, yes, it did," I replied. "But if I don't come up with the canned stuff, he can get pretty nasty about it."

We decided to try the dry-food route but with a much better brand (the most expensive, of course) and see what happens.

Then the vet decided that Spook needed a distemper shot, I practically jumped for joy.

"Great, great," I agreed. "Use a dull needle. Let him know who it feels to get *his* skin punctured for once."

Spook didn't like it at all and, of course, held me totally responsible. I figured I finally beat him at something. I was wrong. A couple of days later we were fighting over the blankets and he managed to inflict a few very nasty slashes on my arm.

I'm fairly used to this and didn't think much about it until I went to my own doctor for an unrelated reason.

She noticed the scratches and asked about them. I assured her they were nothing.

"And when did you have your last tetanus shot?" she asked.

So, guess who got jabbed because of that lousy cat?

If could have been a lot worse, though, this claw-for-a-claw, shot-for-a-shot thing.

After all, I'm the one who had him neutered.

Chapter 8
The Joy of Discipline

I've finally found a way to keep the living-room tiger at bay.

I know, this isn't much a problem with normal house cats, but as I've mentioned time and time again, there's nothing normal about The Spook.

He's a pushy, arrogant, inconsiderate, ungrateful, spoiled, blabber-mouth whose sole purpose in life seems to be harassing me.

And he takes drugs, too. I'd turn him in, but I'm not sure about the illegality of catnip.

Oh, he's mellowed a little since our marriage, but our adversarial situation still hasn't changed a great deal.

The problem, you see, is discipline.

There isn't any.

And, Lord knows, I have certainly *tried*.

I've read those books by so-called cat *therapists* who outline nifty ways to forge meaningful and fulfilling relationships with your animal.

Yeah, right.

Spook shreds these books into confetti.

Let me assure you, I don't hate the cat — I'm just not always real partial to him, particularly when I awake to find him viciously at battle with my arm or leg during one of his frequent predawn attacks.

Still, I'd like to get along, and perhaps, just perhaps, I haven't been treating the saber-toothed midget properly. The problem is that it is difficult to get too affectionate with an animal that has much a lousy disposition.

I've never hit Spooky. That isn't from a lack of trying; it's just that he's too fast. I don't throw things at him either . . . any more. There's nothing more embarrassing than having a smart-alecky cat sneer: "I can throw better than that with one paw tied behind my back."

For awhile, I was able to maintain a smidgeon of discipline with a squirt gun. It worked pretty well at first and, for a time, I was master of the house.

"Spook! You drop my grandchild right now! No? Well, take that!"

Squirt, squirt, squirt. He'd get this wild look on his face, drop whatever he was molesting, and scamper off into the closet.

But the gun has disappeared. I figure he stashed it somewhere.

In any case, I thought possibly I should try to make friends with the beast and try a friendly, rather than adversarial approach.

Let me tell you, it's very difficult to cozy up to a cat who is drenched with suspicion.

I bought a little cat brush. All animals like to be groomed, right?

Not necessarily.

At first he eyed me warily and shivered with apprehension as I gently moved the brush down his back. He let me do this once or twice, then belched out an accusing "meeeaakkk!!!" He chomped down on the brush, whipped it out of my hand, and galloped off. The brush, like the squirt gun, has not been seen since.

This relationship thing wasn't working. What I needed was something we could both relate to, yet keep a proper distance.

I found the perfect solution.

A radio-controlled car. Wow! Why hadn't I thought of this before? To anyone who has a cat, this is a great way to spend some quality time with your animal and still stay out of claw range.

You know what? It works. Spooky is fascinated but leery of the little car that whirrs, spins, bangs into things, and is able to chase him from hiding place to hiding place.

I don't think he's really frightened. When it isn't moving, he'll sneak up on it and bat at the antenna, only to beat a hasty retreat when it goes into motion.

I don't know if all of this is really sane. There are those who accuse me of getting the car as a toy for myself. But this will provide hours of fun for both Spook and me —and teach him a little respect.

He'll never get rid of this. . . now where the hell *is* that thing?

Chapter 9
An Uneasy Peace

Whenever I get desperate for a column I fall back on one of two things — my sex life or my cat. So, we'll talk about the cat — I still *have* a cat.

For those of you who have been faithful readers, you know about The Spook. I saved him from the gas chamber years ago and he has been an ungrateful, pushy, messy, and physically abusive house guest ever since.

After a few violent confrontations, we have generally settled into an uneasy peace. I feed him and he lets me live there.

Now, Spook has a few bad habits and, like everyone else, I have different ways of trying to discipline him, which, as anyone who has a cat can attest, is a joke. I mean, how would you discipline a panther? A chair, whip, and gun would seem appropriate, but there are some fussy animal activists who frown on that.

In the past I've written about some of my methods. The most effective for a while was an old plastic shampoo bottle filled with water. When he misbehaved, like trying to take my foot off because I rolled over on him in bed, I would squirt him with water and he'd run away. That's not so effective any more. Now he squints and ducks, but refuses to move. He knows I don't want to sleep in a wet bed.

I've tried other methods, but the one with the most puzzling effect is when I simply hum. We were lounging on the sofa one day and I began to hum some song from the radio. Spooky popped his head up and his ears flickered and turned sideways. He gaped at me, his eyes fully dilated. He whipped his head toward the window, the door, and back to me. Then, almost clinging to the ground, he rapidly slunk into the bedroom.

I was astonished. The only thing I can figure is that he heard this strange, frightening noise and had no idea where it was coming from. Obviously it wasn't coming from me because my lips weren't moving. I don't use that method too often because it seems kind of unfair.

I've gotten the same effect by blowing into the top of a beer bottle. The whistle totally rattles him.

Since we live in a relative light combative situation (like most married couples). I don't become too concerned with discipline, but I'm always willing to listen to new ideas — although I'm not always sure the professionals have really practical advice.

A recent story quoted an animal behaviorist for the Denver Dumb Friends League. The woman said, "Don't yell at a cat, If you yell or make an angry move, your cat may associate you with the negative consequence..." Well, no kidding. It would seem you'd *want* the cat to know there is a negative consequence when he steals the roast beef off your plate. She suggests a loud noise rather than screaming curses and chasing the cat with a baseball bat.

And she's right. A shotgun blast is much more effective, albeit a tad messy.

She also says that elimination problems are a common complaint with cats. At first I didn't understand that. I mean there are plenty of ways to eliminate a cat.

I read further on, and what she meant was elimination problems with the litter box. So far, The Spook has not had any elimination problems and seems satisfied with his litter box.

But I understand there is a book or pamphlet out now that can show you how to teach your cat to use the toilet, just like people! This seems like it would be a real challenge and I'm going to try it. I'll let you know in a few weeks how this works out. I guess the only problem is how I'm going to get the sand in and out of the toilet.

Finally, our expert suggests that if you are unable to solve your cat training problems, hire a professional behaviorist who will come to your home and diagnose and treat a specific problem for fees ranging from $75 to $200. $75 to $200??!! To have someone tell you how to train a cat that can't be trained anyway? And for a cat that's worth about seven bucks in the first place?

Hey, take a small portion of that fee and buy a whole bunch of cats, and simply keep the one that offends you the least.

Chances are he'll be just like The Spook.

Chapter 10
A Battle of the Brains

I was just reading about a guy who raised the hackles of some dog owners by ranking breeds by their intelligence.

He then put the results in a book entitled *The Intelligence of Dogs: Canine Consciousness and Capabilities*. This particularly provoked owners of the Afghan hound because he rated them dumbest of the 133 canine breeds. On the other hand, the results were applauded by border collie fans; that dog was ranked the smartest.

Cats, however, are a different case. Such studies on cats are meager indeed, the reason being that most cats are too smart to take the tests.

Cats have been called everything from the manifestation of evil to ungrateful wretches . . . and all that is pretty much true. But nobody is ever going to call them stupid.

I know. I have a cat. Spooky is whacky, inconsiderate, selfish, loud, and I think he drinks. But he isn't stupid.

I've had this cat for several years now, and we've had a pretty consistent hate/hate relationship. I often said I'd throw him out but I can't catch him. Yet I don't know how I'd get along without him. We constantly bicker, have no respect for individual privacy, and do our best to upset each other. It's a lot like human relationship's.

Or maybe more appropriately, we are turning into grumpy old men.

This is particularly true with the bed. We have been sharing the same bed for our whole relationship, more or less.

It used to be when we'd have a territorial dispute, I'd give him a shove with my foot and he'd grudgingly move over.

No more. Now he lets out an angry yowl and lashes out. It is no longer a foot — it's a target. This results in a tussle that I eventually win because I'm much bigger. But it's getting tougher and tougher.

Because of my supposedly superior intellect, I should have the upper hand in all spats. But I don't think even a genius could get the better of a cat if they live together long enough.

Cats are very patient. If given enough time, they know they can drive you crazy.

They do this in a very subtle ways. The most popular with Spook is to be constantly in the way but plead innocent when confronted. If I open the door to the refrigerator, he deliberately plants himself in front of it and won't move, even if I threaten to close the door on him. He forces me to scream at him to move, then he retreats with an air of wounded dignity.

Another trick is to beg, plead, and almost grovel to be fed, then immediately turn up his nose at the offering. It later will be gobbled down when I'm not watching.

The only real means I had of getting even with this ingrate was a small squirt gun, which he hated with a passion. It got to be where all I had to do was yell, "I'm gonna get my gun," and he'd scamper for safety.

Now the gun is gone. I don't know where it is, but *he* knows it's gone. When I threaten to get it, he just snickers.

The only other thing he seemed to respect was the vacuum cleaner, but even that's no longer effective. He thinks he killed it.

Every time the vacuum came out, Spooky would run and hide. One day the vacuum was lying idle in the living room. I heard this strange sound and peeked in.

There was The Spook, gingerly slapping at the hose, then leaping back. He did that several times, then crouched down, tail slashing the air, and leaped on the canister, ferociously clutching it in a death grip while his back legs pistoned away, clawing the creature into submission.

He apparently felt that he had killed the beast. It made no more noise and didn't move.

It makes me just a little leery. I'm running out of weapons and the cat is becoming more and more confident.

I could get another squirt gun, I suppose. But I could also get a dog, and together I bet we could outsmart him.

But you can bet it won't be an Afghan. We are definitely talking border collie here.

Chapter 11
The Great Misadventure

The Spook has made his bid for freedom, although I guess it was more like running away.

It was rather surprising. In the years I've had my cantankerous cat, Spook has never taken it on the lam before.

Oh, he's made some pathetic attempts at freedom, but it is all false bravado. The laundry room is right across the hall and when he sees me leave with the laundry basket, he waits next to the door, spurting out into the hallway when I re-enter.

But once he gets out the door, he has no idea where to go. He may have the heart of a lion inside our four walls, but out in the world he has the guts of a chicken. After careening around for a few feet, he meekly hunkers down and lets me pick him up.

I think he does it just to hear me yell at him.

Not exactly an adventurer, he's never even made a real attempt to enter the great outdoors before, so I don't know why he'd want to run away. It certainly isn't as if he is self-sufficient. He'd never be able to catch anything to eat. As cats go, he's an aberration.

They are supposed to be sleek, graceful, and quick with a perfect sense of balance. The Spooker has none of the these traits. He is fat, clumsy, slow, and the only cat I've ever known to land flat on his butt instead of his feet when descending from a high place. And when he does hit the ground, it sounds like a bag of wet cement. All this can be destructive.

The other day, a neighbor cat named Bear stopped by the window to pay his respects. Bear is a nice, friendly cat, but The Spooker would have none of it. He went practically berserk, scrambling up the bookcase to register his rage at this intrusion.

Unfortunately Spook is fat and the ledge is slim. He threw his whole body into an impressive hiss and promptly flipped off the ledge, knocking over the bookcase and winding up in the rubble of books and VCR tapes.

He was baffled for a second but quickly darted on top of the television as another step to the window ledge. Unfortunately, he missed his spot by just a fraction and immediately began to slide down the slanted top of the TV. His eyes went wild with fear and frustration, legs pumping in a cartoon fashion, trying to gain a grip. It was to no avail; he slowly slithered down the back and crashed into the mass of wires behind the set, pulling a few out on the way down.

He was tangled for several moments and, at that point, Bear decided to find a more formidable opponent ... or at least one who could make it to the playing field.

Maybe Spook was looking for a rematch. I don't know, but I went home the other day and he didn't greet me at the door. This is unheard of. I called a few times and checked out his usual hiding places. I figured he was mad at me for something when I noticed that the screen was pushed out. He definitely had flown the coop.

I had mixed emotions about this. I didn't know whether to feel crestfallen or ecstatic.

Should I drown my sorrows or celebrate? I decided the first thing to do was to try to find him. I didn't know whether he'd been gone for hours or just a few minutes. He might be miles away by now, making someone else's life miserable.

I went out into the yard and glanced around. The bushes about 10 feet away rustled slightly and a pair of frightened golden eyes peered anxiously at me.

"Spooker?" I asked. He sprang from the bushes and leaped into my arms, hiding his head in the crook of my elbow, his whole body shaking as he tried to tell me all about his terrifying adventure.

His fur was a bit roughed up, so he might have met Bear and ended up the loser.

I think his career as an escape artist was exciting but short.

It's too bad. I purposely leave the screen unlatched in hopes he might make another bid for freedom, but he hasn't even tried.

I don't suppose you can blame him much.

It's a Bear of a world out there.

Chapter 12
The 'Companion Animal'

This animal-rights movement is getting a little ridiculous.

I always thought I had a pet.

OK, Spook, my cat, is sort of a *nasty* pet, but I consider him a pet nonetheless.

Apparently, according to some animal rights proponents I read about in a story the other day, I do not have a pet.

I have a "companion animal."

Bull. No, I don't have a bull, but my cat is no more my "companion animal" than the Roman Colosseum lion was companion animal to the early Christians.

As I was reading this article, I nudged Spook with my foot.

"Hey, are you my 'companion animal?' '' I asked.

He bit me.

Slapping on a tourniquet to stop the bleeding, I continued to read with fascination. The story also pointed out that the words "owner" or "master" are undesirable.

What the hell are we then? The rights proponents gently suggest "caretaker'' or "guardian," or maybe "steward."

Eh?

Picture this scene: A person asks me if I'm the owner of my cat.

"Goodness no," I reply icily, offended by the suggestion. "I am the *caretaker* of this companion animal."

There is a moment's hesitation, and then he asks, taking a step backwards, "Right ... and, uh, just where is your caretaker?"

And try telling your irate neighbor with the perfectly manicured lawn — a lawn upon which your Great Dane has just taken a big dump — that you are not the dog's owner, but simply a humble caretaker.

"Yeah?" he'll reply, hurling the offensive deposit at you with a shovel,

"Well, take care of *this!*"

Things could get confusing with this "companion" thing.

Just the other night, for instance, I was with this lady of dubious moral integrity, and a friend approached. "Tom, is this your compensated companion for the evening?"

"No," I answered, confused.

"This is my hooker."

I'm really not trying to ridicule those people who obviously are very sincere about creating a greater respect for our furry and feathered friends. I've always been a friend to animals of all kinds (except, of course, for Spook.)

In fact, my admiration and devotion to the animal world ignited some heated reaction recently when I wrote a mild anti-hunting column.

I suppose I will now spark the indignation of animal rights enthusiasts everywhere, but I will forever balk at bestowing human qualities and intelligence upon animals. The term for this is anthropomorphism.

Folks, they aren't human. All the fancy phrasing isn't going to make animals human. And even the most intelligent animal is a dodo by human standards.

The beloved dolphin, which has been hailed as having the closest thing to a human brain since Mick Jagger, isn't all that bright when you get down to it. I mean, if they are so damn smart, how come they keep getting caught up in the nets along with the stupid fish?

If this animal companion thing catches on, does that mean the word "pet" will become outlawed?

Will favored students be known as "teacher's suck-up companions"? And how about the little things that nettle a person — will they be called "aggravation companion peeves"? Will Ann Landers have to change the title of one of her advice booklets to, *Necking, Breast Companioning, and How Far to Go?*

What about pet stores? Will they be called "Companion Animal Emporiums"? I don't think so. In fact, I think the folks advocating these changes are barking up the wrong tree.

Actually, I think the animal rights movement is going to the dogs...whoops!

Make that "companion animals."

Chapter 13
It's Curtains For the Cat

I guess its time for a Spook report.

People have been asking me how my cat, Spook, is getting along. He's been the subject of several spiteful columns, and since I haven't written anything about him in the past few months, the general belief is that I've killed him.

Well, Spook is not dead. In fact, he's recovering nicely since I sat on him. ... and then there was that curtain-rod nastiness. In both cases it was his fault — honest.

The sit-on was pure accident, obviously the result of a move that he hadn't thought all the way through.

Spook has a habit of grabbing any sofa or chair that I've been occupying. I get up for a moment to go to the kitchen, and when I return, he is sprawled in the space, casting a defiant glare in my direction — daring me to shoo him off.

The other day, he moved just a little too fast. I was fiddling with the computer and stood up momentarily to make an adjustment on the back of the monitor. I sat right back down and plunked some 200-plus pounds on a stupid Spooker who had glided into the seat while I was tinkering.

He screamed in outrage and wriggled frantically. I didn't realize I could leap that high in the air without using my legs. We hit the floor about the same time and wound up nose to nose, looking wildly at one another.

I swore at him. He meowled at me, shook himself briefly, then stalked off with an air of injured dignity.

Since he could still walk, I figured he was OK.

I wasn't so sure immediately after the curtain-rod incident.

My apartment is about half subterranean with windows that are about five feet or so from the floor. Like all cats, Spooky enjoys sitting in the window and watching the world go by. He has no problem getting to the ledge in the living room; the TV is in front of it so he has something to climb up on.

In the bedroom, it's a different story. He has to make the leap in one shot, and since he weighs almost as much as I do, this is a formidable task. He's no feline Michael Jordan. He usually makes a big production out of it. Eyeing the ledge intently, he goes into a crouch, wiggles his butt in anticipation, then straightens up and thinks about it. Then repeats the process all again.

This particular night he was even more hesitant than usual, but when I made fun of him, he decided to go for it. He leaped, but his front paws didn't quite gain a grip (he has been declawed on the front but still carries those lethal weapons on the back.) Frantically he scrambled, but his rear paws could not gain any purchase on the plaster wall and he was going down. He frantically twisted his head, his eyes searching madly for something to grasp. Suddenly, he sprang to the side and got a death grip on the curtain.

Now the curtain rod was designed to carry a normal load. This does not cover a 250-pound cat hitting it on the fly.

I watched in awe as the rod groaned slightly, then the anchors shot out of the wall and the whole shebang came crashing to the ground.

I found Spooky in the middle of the debris. It took a few minutes to untangle him, but then he seemed all right. He didn't appreciate the laughing, though.

A more immediate problem was the window. I've always had a bit of the exhibitionist in me, but giving passersby an unobstructed view of my bedroom was going a little far, even for me.

A few towels and thumbtacks temporarily fixed that problem, and the following day, with the help of some impressive heavy operating equipment, I reinstalled the curtain rod.

That isn't going to happen again, believe me. This baby could hold a dangling elephant.

Then again, Spook has been eyeing the contraption with keen speculation.

Maybe I'll add a couple of more heavy-duty screws, just to be on the safe side.

Chapter 14
A Nocturnal Beast

Somebody spilled the beans. My cat has learned the meaning of nocturnal. Even worse, he knows now that he is it.

This has stirred up some problems in an already pretty chaotic relationship.

I don't know who told him. Maybe he's been watching *National Geographic* behind my back or something. But all these years I've told him that cats are just like humans. They stay up during the day and sleep during the night. The only nocturnal things were disgusting animals like bats and hookers. He certainly didn't want to associate himself with anything like *them* did he?

So I've had him buffaloed for many years. Then out of nowhere, something feral clicked on inside his fevered brain. He somehow felt the call of the nocturnal wild. He echoed this call about 3 a.m. a couple of weeks ago. This is not the greatest way, not to mention time, to get roused from a deep sleep.

He figures since he's up, then it must be time for breakfast, and guess who the waiter is.

The first time was really horrifying. I felt this dampness against my face and when I opened my eyes, all I could see were these glowing eyes staring accusingly at me. We were nose to nose — a sort of feline hound of the Baskervilles.

The first couple of times I thought it was just a fluke. Maybe his internal clock had gone a little haywire for a while. I tried to ignore him, figuring he'd go away. No luck. He's very persistent. When nudging me with his nose doesn't work, he begins to slap me, meowing all the time, "Hey, HEY. Get up!"

I tried pulling the covers over my head, and that seemed to stymie him for a while. Then he discovered the phone. No, he doesn't call me. But, he does yank the phone off the stand, and after a few moments a voice keeps telling me to hang the thing up.

Since I'm not eager to join these 3 a.m. parties, I've tried to discourage them through cunning. When he wakes me I make a big production out of getting out of bed and lumbering toward the kitchen. He skips along beside me and as soon as we leave the bedroom I leap back in and close the door. Then I go back to bed.

Oddly enough, smart as he is, he falls for this almost all the time. Occasionally he'll balk at the door, and I have to actually walk into the kitchen before he can't stand it anymore and comes galloping in. Even though I guess by now he knows he's going to be tricked, he still forges hopefully ahead, kind of like Charlie Brown and his football.

He doesn't like it when he's duped. First he yowls loudly and hurls himself against the door. Now a 250-pound cat (okay, a slight exaggeration) can create an impressive thud. When that doesn't work he goes in the kitchen and bangs the cabinet doors.

Eventually he settles down, but I've been trying to find a better alternative. Lately I've been trying to turn the tables on him. Since he won't let me sleep at night, I won't let him sleep during the daytime. it seems like a fair trade. It isn't easy keeping a cat awake when he doesn't want to be. Oh, yeah, I can jostle him around, but after biting me, he can drop back off to sleep in an instant. So I've discovered a way to have him keep at least one eye open at all times. I sneak up and goose him when he least expects it.

He really hates that and is afraid to completely fall asleep because he doesn't know when or where I'll strike. For instance, he'll be dozing on the sofa and I'll sneak out of the kitchen.

Slowly, slowly, I creep and stalk up on him and then suddenly tweak him on the stem of the tail. The results are spectacular. I've even gotten a complete flip.

But it doesn't work much anymore. Now, anytime I'm even in the house he's on the alert. Even if his eyes are closed, he's not really sleeping. And boy, does he have magnificent hearing. I can be halfway across the room when he'll suddenly stiffen and twist his head around to look at me. I suppose it would work better if my knees didn't creak every now and then to give me away.

So far this hasn't been the right solution. We still have our 3 a.m. roustings. Maybe I should trade him in for a bat.

Or a hooker.

Chapter 15
Things That Go Plump In The Night

I awoke in a clammy sweat. I knew I was not alone in that pitch-black bedroom. Lurking somewhere in that blackened pit was a creature of unspeakable evil.

I could barely hear a whisper of sound as the creature crept ever closer. I could imagine its sleek muscles bunching up for the final leap. I squinted my eyes in the darkness and saw two flaring gold eyes, burning with a frightful ferocity. I could imagine the gleaming fangs, jutting from a mouth salivating with anticipation. I thought of running, but it was too late. In an instant, the creature launched itself at me, eyes blazing, jaws agape, and claws bared to tear and shred.

He charged onto the bed and thrust his face directly in front of mine, but before I could scream, he belched "Meeoooowwwr?"

Not many cats in this world get so dramatic when simply asking for breakfast.

The first time it happened, it scared me half to death. I knew something, or someone, was in the room and I was practically paralyzed with fear. But it turned out to be none other than my old Spooker cat. With a new trick.

Unfortunately, Spook has discovered food.

It isn't that I haven't fed him during the years we've been together. It's just that he didn't know there was anything but the cheap, dry stuff — you know, it costs about 75 cents a box and looks the same as the other food that costs a buck or more.

Ever since he was a kitten, I gave him whatever was cheapest, and he figured that's the way it was. Oddly enough, he never ever cared for people food. He seemed to prefer the cheap stuff. Maybe he figured that anything I ate couldn't be any good.

Things were fine until a few months ago, when he fell under the bad influence of another cat, one that was fed from a can each morning and evening

— in addition to having a continuing supply of dry food.

The first time he watched her being fed, he shot me an offended look as if to say, "Hey, what the hell is going on here?"

I told him he didn't like canned food, but he insisted on trying. I still don't think he cared much for it. But he gobbled it each day, anyway. The reason for this was not hunger, it was greed. If he didn't pounce on it immediately, the other cat sneaked over and wolfed it down.

That's the way it worked until we became bachelors again. I figured we'd go back to the old ways. That lasted until about 5:30 a.m. the second morning. I awoke to this strange shuffling around the room and a sudden pouncing on the bed.

When I regained my calm, his face was directly in mine and he was quite vocal about the fact that I hadn't been giving him his twice daily canned-food ration.

Nobody, not even a mother, can inflict guilt on a person like a wronged cat.

I shoved him off the bed — at his weight this is no simple task — and rolled over.

I had an uncomfortable feeling and opened my eyes. There, peeping over the edge of the bed was the disapproving face of the Spooker. His accusing eyes were accompanied by a weak, pitiful squeak; a nice touch, I thought.

It would have taken a harder heart than mine to refuse this impressive appeal. There was only one problem. I didn't *have* canned cat food. I did, however, have some tuna fish.

What a treat! I thought! Watch, he'll gobble this stuff and expect no less in the future.

Wrong again.

He took one sniff and glared at me as if to say, "What is this crap? You can't fool me with this trash. I want the real cat food: you know, ground up fish innards, noses, and eyeballs."

And with that he flounced off, leaving the food untouched.

So, I now have a supply of cheap canned cat food. I don't think he really cares that much for it, but habits are hard to break. And I don't forget very often, either.

Because when I do, I get a 5 a.m. visitor.

Chapter 16
Spooky is Litter-ally On Top

There is much to be said for the placement of a litter box.

Unfortunately, not a great deal is actually said about this rather touchy subject, but it is an integral part of life for those who happen to have a cat.

Since I have a cat I have a deep interest in this subject, because it can be the source of some uncomfortable situations.

The very, very first thing one does after getting a cat is get a litter box. If you don't you will probably be wondering why you got the cat in the first place.

The box is a simple contraption. Mine is an old turkey roaster pan filled with litter that sort of clots, allowing me to clean everything out once a day. If I forget this little duty, the cat will quickly remind me by depositing his little duty on the carpet.

The next thing is very important: placement.

The ideal place is a basement. It's out of the way and most basements have monsters that might eat the cat if you are lucky. But, since I live in a one-bedroom apartment, I don't have that option.

At first I thought the best spot would be the bathroom. After all, it was created for that particular function.

I had read that some people have trained cats to use the toilet. I thought this a marvelous idea. In fact, I spend not a little time trying to get Spooky to learn this wonderful trick. I came to the conclusion that people who claim their cats use the toilet also claim weekly visits to Mars.

I don't think a cat can be trained. In fact, in most cases the cat is the trainer ... not the trainee. I guess we both failed. He had absolutely no interest in indulging in the toilet and he couldn't get me to use the litter box.

It was a standoff.

I also abandoned the bathroom idea because I found that a litter box is not fun to discover while stumbling about in the dark in the middle of the night.

This pretty well cut down my options.

There was the kitchen, but I didn't think that was a good idea. The roaches might complain.

Finally I settled on an area right outside the kitchen because it was a good distance from the living room area where I spend most of my time. This worked until I bought a dining-room table and placed it, unfortunately, next to the litter box. I didn't realize that was a problem until I had a few friends over to play poker.

The Spook likes people and was fascinated with this group. He doesn't really know he's a cat and the first thing he did was let it be known that he wanted to join in the game.

I threw him off the table and he sulked a bit, then seemed satisfied to sit in one of the vacant chairs and watch the play with keen interest, slapping at a stray chip every now and then.

When a late arrival came in, The Spook wasn't at all willing to give up his seat. Finally I had to shove him off and he struck back in a very underhanded way.

"Whewwwww!" One guy exploded, throwing his hand over his nose. "What in the hell is that stink?"

Well, it was Spooky registering his unhappiness in the most odious way imaginable.

Everyone began turning a bit green and even though I ran around with a room freshener spray, things just weren't the same after that and the game broke up early.

This pointed up my dilemma. I didn't have anywhere else to put the thing.

But, I did manage to solve the problem. From now on, we just let Spooky play cards with us. He's a lousy player anyway ... he always purrs when he has a good hand.

And that sure beats the alternative.

Chapter 17
You Want How Much??

It's time to change my habitat. And it puts me into a quandary because I am faced with a big decision: to boot The Spook or shell out some big bucks for a cantankerous cat. What to do?

This problem popped up when my current neighborhood started getting a bit too exciting for my taste and the prospect of boredom was looking real attractive. So I launched a search for another place.

There are a lot of apartments for rent in Toledo. The classified section of The Blade has columns and columns of them, and I thought that finding a new place wouldn't be a problem.

Wrong.

Oh, there were plenty of appealing places for rent, but they all had one slight hang-up. They didn't want my cat.

I suppose you can't blame them. I don't really want him all that much, but after several years, I've gotten used to him. It's kind of like the gout. You don't like it, but it certainly gets your attention.

There were places that would take the cat, but, unfortunately, they didn't want me.

Finally, I found a delightful utopia in this neat apartment complex. Quiet, dignified, air conditioned, in a venue that offers a swimming pool, and conveniently located near stores, eating establishments, and a lot of potential pick-up bars.

All went well until I asked about the cat. The young woman told me that cats require a $200 deposit.

$200!

I blinked a few times. $200? That's ridiculous. Spook doesn't have anywhere near that amount in his savings account. That's when it hit me that I was supposed to put up the money. I began to babble.

"Look," I pointed out. "That cat isn't worth $200. Hey, when I stupidly

41

bailed him out of death row four years ago it only cost me $30 or $40 and I've been bemoaning that ever since. . .Why, for $200 I can buy a lot better companionship than him — maybe just for the evening, but a lot better."

She was polite but firm. Those are the rules.

I tried the intimidation route.

"This smacks of discrimination to me," I warned. "Let's face it, I bet you don't charge a $200 deposit for kids, and they would cause a lot more damage than him."

A polite shrug.

"Also, he's been 'fixed'. I betcha there's a law against charging an extra deposit for cats with an alternative life-style."

This didn't make any sense even to me, so I switched tactics. I decided to play on Spooky's notoriety. "Perhaps you don't know it, but his is one of the most famous cats in Toledo," I boasted. "Perhaps you've read about him in my column. This would probably be a great selling point in your promotions."

Yes, she knew who Spooky was, and no, the rules aren't changed for anybody, famous or not. Well, that's what they say, but I'll bet if Morris or Socks wanted to rent an apartment there would be some rule bending.

I read the lease and Spooky almost got nailed on weight. There is a 25-pound limit and that's about what he weighs now . . . that's $8 a pound. That's more than prime rib! I pointed all this out very carefully.

However, all this whining didn't have much effect.

Now, this is a rough decision. It really shouldn't be, because I used to shake my head in pity at people who spend large sums of money on their pets.

I know a lawyer who told me he had just spend $300 on his diabetic dog. I thought this was outrageous. Nobody should spend that kind of money on an animal.

And now I'm faced with coming up with $200 for a cat — and he isn't even sick!

I really can't think of any sane reason to spend that kind of money on this lousy old cat who doesn't even like me.

But, you know what?

I will.

Chapter 18
Spending quality time

One of those pet books advised the reader to "spend some quality time with your cat."

I was having some very dark thoughts about this statement while gently dabbing some iodine on the latest assortment of scratches inflicted on me by Spooky, a cross between a puma and a grizzly bear who masquerades as an ordinary house cat.

I've often written about The Spook and, judging from the response, he's a very popular fellow. This is surprising because he is a very nasty and ungrateful bully. And, he likes to scratch me.

That's *his* idea of quality time.

Also, he's a vandal. He opens kitchen cabinets and throws things on the floor. He spills his water dish, knocks pictures off the bookcase, and grabs the end of the toilet paper roll and streams it throughout the house.

He also screams at me. For no reason, he will loudly caterwaul, and if I could understand catonese, I'm sure I'd be told off good and proper.

A friend, who knows absolutely nothing about cat psychology (therefore is an expert), asked if I ever show him any attention.

"Attention? Why, hell yes, I show him attention. When he knocked my third-place golf trophy off the bookcase, I chased him all over the house with a fly swatter. Of course I didn't hit him. I didn't even get close, but, by God, he sure got some attention *that* day."

"No, no," she said. "I mean like affection or playing with him."

I thought about that for a moment. "When he yowls at me until it drives me nuts, I have this bottle bag filled with water that I squirt at him and it generally results in a sullen silence. That's sort of like playing."

She shook her head sadly. then she went into this "quality time" stuff, showing affection, you know, like petting him.

I figured I'd give it a try.

When I approached him, Spooky was suspicious. Since I wasn't carrying a fly swatter or a water bottle bag, he let me get close, but he was ready for flight or fight at the wrong move.

I began to pet him.

He looked at me incredulously, and then his eyes softened. He slumped down and rolled over on his back. There was a slight snarling sound that is as close as he can get to a purr.

Oh, wow. This was going to work. He wanted me to rub his belly.

Right. And do you know *why* he wanted his belly rubbed?

I'll tell you. It was because then he could entrap my arm with his front legs, bite down hard on my hand, and pump his lethal back legs like a rabbit, ripping my arm to shreds.

Before I could even react, he suddenly released me and galloped away, laughing nastily.

Although I had all the excuse in the world, I didn't kill him. Nor did I give up on quality time.

We now play a little game that's great fun. I know I enjoy it and I don't think he hates it too much.

Whenever I want to spend some time with Spook, I "sock" him.

No, no, I don't hit him. I take one of my socks and pull it over his head.

Of course it's not one of my dirty socks. That would be cruel and unusual punishment.

The reaction to being "socked" is amazing.

Spooky never attempts to pull the sock off. He simply tries to back out of it which, of course is impossible. He winds up running in circles backwards. With the toe of the sock flapping back and forth, he resembles a cute baby elephant running in reverse.

Now before the letters of anger start pouring in, let me say that Spooky isn't in any pain. I think it might be a bit embarrassing to him because I laugh so hard I fall off the sofa, but I don't think he minds it too much. I never leave it on for more than a few hours and he generally comes back for more. If he offers any resistance, while I'm pulling it over his head, I stop.

There's always another day and I've got plenty of socks.

You know, this quality time thing isn't so tough after all.

Or, as Spook might say, "Sock it to me."

Chapter 19
Finally, a use for the cat

I've finally found a use for the cat.

Cats are, for the most part, useless. Unless you have mice. Or a masochistic urge for abuse. Oh, sure, there are the general reasons to keep a feline around — using one of his claws to clean fingernails, for instance. But I have discovered that my cat can perform a truly valuable service, particularly since I'm prone to absent-mindedness.

You've heard of Seeing-Eye dogs, right? Well, I have a seeing-memory cat. I know that sounds silly, but it's true. I have a couple of examples here that illustrate that my memory is not what it used to be and that The Spooker knows what to do about it. This is especially true if food is involved.

The other morning I woke up and groggily stumbled into the kitchen to feed the cat. This has top priority. It is the first thing that must be done even before scratching oneself.

Spook is very vocal. He prods, whines, cajoles, and keeps up a steady patter of impatient scolding from the moment my feet hit the floor until he's munching on breakfast.

I opened a can, scooped out a generous dollop, plopped it in his dish, then went into the bathroom to perform my daily ablutions. Suddenly I felt this frantic pawing at my leg. Spook had a desperate look on his face and was literally screaming at me while he attempted to physically drag me from the bathroom.

I couldn't figure out what was wrong. Maybe he didn't like that particular food. Tough. You have to draw the line somewhere. Still, he was so persistent, I went to find out what the trouble was.

That's when I saw why he was so upset. I put the food in the dish, all right, but instead of putting the dish on the floor, I put it in the refrigerator.

He cursed me until I put it on the floor and still managed to grumble between bites. "I'm never going to be able to train this moron," he seemed to say.

The other situation was somewhat more serious.

I came home from work and proceeded to give Spook his dinner, another high priority item. Every day, I am met at the door and led to the refrigerator under a constant barrage of mews and meows, telling me how his day went.

I put his food down (on the floor) and started the water to wash the dishes (a ritual required when there are no clean dishes left anywhere in the house.)

I went into the bedroom to change clothes, then wandered into the living room and turned on the television, the highlight of my average day. (The excitement can get overwhelming sometimes.)

While watching the tube the peace was shattered by a concerned yowl.

I looked over and The Spook had stopped eating and was staring into the kitchen. He looked back at me with a pleading look and yowled again. He repeated this several times, wagging his paw in an anxious gesture.

I tried to ignore him, so he came trotting over and began pawing at my leg with a desperate frenzy.

Finally I hauled myself up from the sofa and went into the kitchen to discover, to my horror, that the faucet was still running, overflowing the sink and cascading to the floor.

Had it not been for the persistence of Spook, the flooding could have been the worst thing since Johnstown flood. As it was, there was no damage (hear that landlord?) and it took only a few minutes to sop up the spill. This was all done under the supervision of Spook who seemed to be saying, "You idiot. Where would you be without me?" Strangely enough, this was a popular statement from my ex-wife ... and ex-girlfriend ... and ex-drill instructor ... and ex-mother. Hey, who needs any of those people when you have a cat?

So, now I have a new appreciation for Spook. In fact, as a reward, I gave him a bath the other day.

And he really enjoyed it, too. There was one drawback though. I really hate the way the fur sticks to your tongue.

But, that's OK. I'm sure to forget it.

Chapter 20
Hide and Squeak

My life with Spook gets a little goofier all the time.

There are two things that he really excels at that drive me nuts: hiding and closing doors.

Both can be very frustrating and, of course, that's the reason he does it.

Hiding, for instance.

As anyone who owns a cat can tell you, there isn't any cubby hole too small to squeeze into ... even if that cat weighs 250 pounds (which is Spooky's weight, give or take a couple of ounces.)

When it comes to hiding, timing is everything, and The Spook has it down to a clever science.

He realizes there is no sense in hiding if I'm not looking for him. There isn't a great deal of fun in that.

No, he waits until I've left the door open for some reason or another. Usually it's when I'm doing my laundry. The washer is right across the hall, so I sometimes forget to close the door when I go out there, knowing I'll be back shortly.

This is one of his greatest moments.

He knows I saw him standing by the door when I left. So that's when he pulls his disappearing act.

I come back in and he's not there. Now I'm *certain* he didn't scoot out the door and gallop off somewhere in the building. But, I'm not *positive* he didn't. So that means I have to either search the building or the apartment to find him.

Now this isn't a problem with a dog. Dogs are kind of dumb. You just whistle and the dog comes, forgetting he was playing a game. You can whistle, jump up and down, holler, and offer all sorts of catnip treats, and a cat won't budge.

So, you have to launch a search. This is tough enough as it is, but when you have a cat the color of midnight, you can skip right by him in a darkened closet or cabinet.

And you can believe he knows this.

It may not seem likely, but I'm willing to bet he holds his breath and closes his eyes whenever I'm near his little cranny.

It usually take quite a while before I finally find him and the whole procedure can start all over again when I go out to use the drier.

One time he outsmarted himself. I searched high and low — even in the refrigerator — and couldn't find a trace of him.

Finally I gave up, figuring he'd drop in from somewhere eventually or find his way home if he did, in fact, slip out of the building.

Much later I heard this rather pitiful meowing. I had a hard time tracking down the muffled noise until I discovered he had somehow gotten behind the water heater in the closet.

Getting him out was not going to be simple. The heater is jammed in tight and the only way behind it is over the top and that is blocked pretty well with pipes.

I couldn't get my arm through there to reach him on the other side.

It seemed like the only way to get him out was to disconnect and move the water heater. This would be a major job, quite honestly above my abilities. This would mean having the maintenance people at the apartment complex do it. I bet this wouldn't be cheap.

In fact, it would be a lot more expensive than a new cat. I thought about that for awhile but figured if I *didn't* get him out, he would start to smell after a few days.

Suddenly, dullard that I am, I got an idea. I grabbed a towel and slid it over the top and down the back of the heater. After a few moments, Spooky caught on, grabbed onto the towel and I pulled him out of his trap.

Of course there was no gratitude involved. He just shook himself and looked at me as if to say, "You would never have found me if I hadn't spoken up."

Oh, yeah, another little trick he's learned is that he can close the bathroom door. He waits until about three or four a.m. goes into the bathroom, and slams the door shut.

He does this so he can pretend the door shut itself, trapping him in there forcing him to bleat and yowl about his life-threatening dilemma until I finally get up and open the door. It's all a big sham just to harass me.

I know this, because he's alone in the house all day and *never* gets caught in the bathroom ... just in the middle of the night when I'm sleeping.

I'm beginning to think that I should teach him a lesson by turning the tables on him.

Then again, I don't know how I would ever get out from behind the water heater.

You can bet he wouldn't throw me a towel.

Chapter 21
Shame and Disgrace

Oh, the shame of it all.

Humiliation. Disgrace. Scandal. It was all there.

I'm not talking about President Clinton either. I'm talking about my cat, Spook.

This was supposed to be his big year at the annual household pet cat show, Cavalcade of Cats, held Sunday at Gladieux Plaza.

I was sure he was going to take first this year. In the first two years, we copped two fifths, a third, and a second-place. This time we were shooting for gold.

And we had an edge. Spook was the big-name celebrity of the show. (Not too difficult, seeing as Toledo has precious few famous cats.) He was named official spooksperson. They even had 10 beautiful ribbons called the Spook's Choice Awards! He was to pick 10 lucky cats for the award.

I had brushed and preened him daily. His coat glistened. He was beautiful. We couldn't lose.

And what did this famous, comely, personable, famous cat do?

He attacked the judge, that's what he did.

It was unbelievable. Here I was, grooming a champion, and I wind up with Mike Tyson.

Oh, Spook didn't try to gnaw off the judge's ear, but he did make several credible attempts to take his arm off.

When we got to the show and he was in his home cage, he hissed at his neighbors. But that wasn't what bothered me. What had me worried were the eyes. They were completely dilated and I could see anger smoldering like hot embers.

Still, he seemed to be tolerating things OK. As usual, a lot of wonderful people stopped by to see him, just because they wanted to meet the cat they read about. He generally ignored them. He doesn't handle celebrity well. Sort of like Sean Penn.

Although I had a feeling things weren't right, I shrugged it off. Once he got to the ring, he'd be fine.

Wrong!

When his number was called, I put him in the ring cage along with the other cats and he seemed fine, sniffing and probing the small cage, waiting for his turn.

He was second to be judged and that's when the fun began.

The guy reached in and Spook recoiled, peeled back his lips to show formidable fangs, and hissed a warning. It was scary. He looked like some evil character in a Stephen King novel. I knew I shouldn't have let him watch "Storm of the Century" last week.

The man made several attempts to calm him, but Spook wasn't cooperating. The judge motioned me to come up to the ring and when I got there, I told him that Spook wouldn't bite him. He had never bitten anyone, except me, of course.

"Well, if you say so," he said unconvinced, and tried again. Spook snarled and definitely tried to bite him.

I decided to give it a shot and he went into a fit of anger, screaming, hissing, spitting, and throwing a series of impressive rights. This was all done to the delight of the audience, which had been kind of bored.

Finally, I wrestled him out of the ring cage and returned him to his home cage, where he slunk to the back to lie down and glare at me with those unforgiving eyes.

Well, that was it. I withdrew him from further competition, put him in his carrier, and we left without fanfare, slinking out the door in disgrace.

He was sullen until he got out of his carrier at home. Then he was the old Spook again. He crawled up onto my lap and licked my hand. I guess it was his way of apologizing.

So, all is normal in the household, and Spook is now retired from active competition. He's much happier that way.

Still, it's a real shame. I really wanted that ribbon. Just wait until he tries to put me in a show. I'm going for the ear.

Chapter 22
The Evil That Cats Do ...

As the Bard once said, "The evil that men do lives after them ..."

I suppose that would be true for most of us. Unless you happen to be President.

Or a cat.

In cases such as those, the most outrageous, outlandish, shocking, and obnoxious acts seem to have no bad effects upon the perpetrators. On the contrary, they actually seem to flourish and profit by their misdeeds.

I know. I happen to live with a cat who has become some sort of hero by his treachery.

I have reported how my cat, Spook, behaved horribly at a pet housecat show where he was guest of honor. It began with sulking and pouting and degenerated into hissing and spitting and generally unruly behavior toward anyone who tried to approach him.

This all culminated when he attacked the judge. I tried to intervene, and Spook went on to attack me verbally and physically. With humiliation and embarrassment, I withdrew him from the competition and we went home under a cloud of shame.

At least I did. Spook could not have cared less, even when I told him that his popularity would suffer by these unsavory actions.

Wrong.

Within a week or so after the debacle, Spook received letters of support, gifts, and even ribbons supposedly from his fellow cats and their designated humans who have turned him into some sort of feline hero for spitting in the face of decency and decorum.

It seems kind of hard to believe.

It is even stranger to find that letters addressed to Spook c/o The Blade get delivered to me. I don't get any mail, but that silly cat sure does.

One person was a great fan. A box arrived for Spook and in it was a blue ribbon and a handsome food dish inscribed with the words, "Cat From Hell." An accompanying card read:

"It is with deep admiration and, yes, earned respect that this blue ribbon is presented to you. Admiration for your devilish and disquieting exploits, and respect for a cat, such as yourself, to coexist with a room-mate of such dubious character. The words inscribed on this prize feeding dish will be a daily reminder for all to read or take the consequences of foolhardy actions."

Instead of being vilified, he's being honored.

And that's just the tip of the kitty iceberg.

There were other letters but the one that really took the catnip was one that had a beautiful ribbon attached that proclaimed "Grand Prize Winner."

This was really something as it was allegedly sent by his peers and declared "Spook Ensign" to be the "Grand Champion of the Household Pet Cat Shows 1997-99."

Now how's that for proper punishment?

It went on, "With pen in paw, we felines of the Cavalcade of Cats Show 1999 do declare Spook Ensign to be the greatest V.I.P. (Very Important Purrson.)"

I finally got an obscure mention in the next paragraph:

"We appreciate his and his human's effort to be our spookspurrson, guest judge, fellow participant, and publicist whose vocal comments we fully understood and empathize with ... We shall long remember our V.I.P."

And it was signed with 83 cats' names ranging from Ink-adink-adoo to Baby Piglet. Oh, yeah, it also was framed in various paw prints.

Now, I ask you, is this the proper public reaction for such arcane and despicable behavior? In these times I guess so.

All this has given me a different perspective on things.

I won't enter him in the show next year. I'm afraid he will be far too busy for that.

You see, I'm running him for President.

Chapter 23
Grumpy Old Man

Boy, talk about cranky.

You know how some people when they grow older become a bit more cantankerous? Well, it's the same thing with cats. Catankerous?

At least that's the story with my cat, Spook.

What a grouch.

Right now he's really sore at me, and I'd have to admit he has some justification. But I did apologize, after all. What can I say after I've said I'm sorry?

It was just an accident.

I walked into my darkened bedroom and saw what I thought was a shirt lying on the floor in front of the closet. Without thinking, I tried to kick it into the dirty-clothes basket.

Imagine my surprise when the shirt let out a bellow of outrage.

Talk about mad. He let out a stream of kitty obscenities, and if he had the physical ability, I know he would have called the Humane Society with a loud complaint of abuse.

I tried to explain what happened but he was having none of it. He's being very dramatic about the whole thing.

He sulks and pouts and cringes when I walk into the room. He also gives me The Look. Most of you know what The Look is. At least all men who ever had a mother or a wife knows The Look.

Actually the poor guy had had a really bad day and that clothes-basket thing was just the final insult.

Earlier the grandchildren came over for a visit.

Spook has never been thrilled with the kids. He tolerates them but usually makes himself scarce when they are around, mainly because he doesn't like hugs. I believe he thinks a hug, or any other physical show of affection, is sissy and he wants none of it.

Oh, he'll let me brush him or scratch his ears or back, but no hugs.

Of course, the kids really aren't too concerned with what he wants and go ahead and hug him anyway.

He tries to frighten them but to no avail. Ever since he found he could bully that judge at the cat show by hissing at him, he thinks that he can frighten anyone with it. The kids aren't intimidated at all. In fact, they try to imitate him, much to his chagrin. He's all talk (except for me, of course, whom he bites and scratches with alarming frequency).

So he's been grumpy, but I've been kind of making it up to him.

You see, I had a full-length glass storm door and he would spend hours lying in front of it and surveying what he considers his domain. This is a mixed pleasure. The squirrels, birds, and even a rabbit seem to know he is imprisoned behind the glass and can't get to them. They love to taunt him and he responds with shouts and curses.

He always has to tell me about the interlopers. Once I was taking a shower and he came in the bathroom to tell me about the latest transgressions.

Recently, I had a new storm door installed and the glass only goes halfway down. Spook was immediately upset. He could no longer sit and view the great outdoors. He was quite put out with me about the whole thing.

So, I took one of the kitchen chairs and put it in front of the door. He immediately hopped up and was once again in charge of his domain.

The trouble is, I can't leave it there because it gets in the way. So I just put it over to the side when it's not in use and when he decides he wants to have a look-see, he simply jumps up onto the chair and stares at me with The Look until I come over and carry the chair, with him solidly in place, and put it in front of the door.

I realize some people would say I am spoiling him rotten, and that would probably be true.

But, the way I see it, I'm doing penance. And I really don't mind.

In fact, I'm not kicking at all.

Chapter 24
How to Screw Up Your Cat's Mind

The subject today is how you can get some great enjoyment out of messing with your cat's mind.

This isn't as easy as you might imagine, particularly if you and your feline have been roommates for 10 years as my cat, Spook, and I have been.

We have gotten to know each other pretty well, and while we don't particularly like each other, we're stuck with each other.

Over the years it's been a long trail of one-upmanship and ways to tease or try to drive the other nuts.

Spook's ploys are simple, yet very effective.

I can give you some examples and if you have a household cat, I'll bet you know exactly what I'm talking about.

Each morning when I walk down the hallway from the bedroom to the kitchen, I have a little furry escort. But he's not content with simply following along. Nor is there any inclination to walk alongside.

No, he must walk in front. But he must walk at a very slow pace, forcing me to try to get around him. Hah. Therein lies the trap. You see, he criss-crosses back and forth in front of me, forcing me to trip and stumble to keep from stepping on him.

This is an important part of the game. If I do accidentally nudge him slightly, this is a great bonus. He screeches loudly in outraged dignity and spins around to glare in injured disapproval.

Whenever I am in the kitchen puttering about, he lies as close as he can to my feet and stretches way out so it is almost impossible not to make some contact. And the slightest touch brings out a yowl of protest. As I am usually lost in my thoughts, this noisy intrusion startles the pants off me and I leap into the air with a pretty good yelp myself.

I come down cursing and yelling and he, now content that he has accomplished his goal, trots merrily into the other room.

I am always looking for little ways to get even. Recently I discovered a neat trick to drive him just a little bit nuttier. And I will pass it on to you.

I changed my schedule.

You see, cats are very much creatures of habit and Spook is no exception.

He also has a sense of duty. I normally get up at 8 a.m. and if I don't do that, he is in the bedroom meowing and prodding, bumping me with his head and slapping me on the shoulder. This keeps up until I rise, trip over him down the hall, and put some food in his dish.

Recently, I have been working at a different job at The Blade. (No, this column isn't my only task here, as many seem to think.) It requires me at times to get up at 4 a.m.

Talk about head games. I got up and wandered down the hall. Spook was curled up on the sofa and gave me only a passing glance. I often rise during the night to answer a call of nature, a task that gets a lot more frequent as I grow older.

But imagine his surprise when I kept right on going past him and into the kitchen and started to make breakfast.

He was confused. He just peered around the corner and looked at me questioningly. When I went into the bathroom for my daily ablutions, he mewed in bewilderment. As I put on my clothes, he sat in the doorway and watched me carefully.

I went out the door and he stood at the window, waiting for me to shout, "April Fool!" or something.

This is great. I finally have him totally fouled up. Since then I've been changing the times around, anywhere from 4 a.m. to 8 a.m. just to keep him off balance. And it's working. He doesn't know when to get up or when I'm actually getting up or just visiting the bathroom.

So I think I'll just keep it up for awhile. Actually this is probably more fun than a real life, anyway.

Chapter 25
The Call of The Wild

I have heard the call of the wild, and it isn't pleasant.

Well, actually, I didn't hear it, but my cat, Spook, did, and it resulted in a battle to be remembered. At least by us.

In all the time I've had him, this miserable excuse for a cat has slashed my arms and various other parts of my body, but it was always during our times of roughhouse play. It sometimes got a bit bloody (me, not him) but it was all in good fun, never really serious.

The other day, things changed.

It was my fault, I suppose. Let me give a little advice here: If you have a 10-year-old cat who has never been outside to run loose, keep it that way. There apparently is something about this new-found freedom that can turn a relatively tame kitty into a violent, vicious beast who will turn on you like a wounded bear.

I was just trying to do the guy a favor. Since we moved into our new house and have a big yard, he has been begging to go outside and explore it. I've been leery about this, but I've occasionally let him out, with me close at hand, for a moment or two, and he seemed OK.

So I decided to increase his time. I let him out the other day while I was doing some chores around the yard. I kept my eye on him, and things seemed fine.

Then I tried to take him back inside.

With his new-found confidence, Spook kept avoiding me, staying just out of reach without actually running away. After several minutes of this, I was getting a little annoyed.

While he was sniffing a bush, I sneaked over and picked him up. That's when I discovered he had heard the call of the wild.

You would have thought I rammed him with a hot poker. He yowled in protest and began squirming and hissing.

"Hey, knock it off," I warned and hoisted him up. He went berserk. He was a ball of fury, biting and slashing at my arms. We wrestled like this for several moments as I tried to get a grip on the back of his neck. It was all to no avail.

I finally let him go, expecting him to run away (and at this point I wasn't against it), but instead he whipped around to face me and actually GROWLED. This was no longer a cat. This was a panther. And he was mad. He came after me as if I were a cat-show judge.

I was getting pretty hot myself. "You turn on ME?" I shouted. "Me, who suffered through 14 hours of labor to give you birth?" (This isn't really true. However, it is a line that often served my mother well. Being neutered, Spook knows little about biological inaccuracies.)

We sparred for quite a while longer. Finally I opened the garage/rec-room door and walked into the house to attend my wounds. I watched from the window as he slowly wandered into the garage. I ran out and closed the door. I decided to give him a half hour to chill out a bit.

I then returned to the garage and found him sulking on a window ledge. I tried to approach him in a friendly, cajoling way and when I got close, the ungrateful little hairball bared his teeth and spit at me.

I'm not really proud of what happened next. I got so annoyed I spit back, right in his face. He didn't blink. That did it for me. I went out, got his food, water, and litter box, tossed them in the garage, and told him, "Fine. You can just spend the night out here."

Despite my resolve, after three hours, I crept into the garage to find him lying by the door. I gingerly picked him up and he emitted a half-hearted hiss but took no further action.

I carried him into the house where he underwent a magical transformation. He was my buddy Spook again. When I sat down, he hopped into my lap and apologized profusely for his tasteless behavior. He had no idea what came over him. He promised it would never happen again.

And it won't, either. He is never going out again. I've heard the call of the wild and find it spooky.

Chapter 26
Hair Balls and Other Fancy Stuff

If you want to put a negative thrill in your life, try giving your cat a pill. The degree of difficulty is one step above trying to put toothpaste back into the tube.

I was reminded of this recently when I was given not one, but a whole bottle of pills to be administered to my cat, Spook.

Oddly enough, throughout the 10 years we've been together, I have rarely had to give him any medication. He's been an extremely healthy cat. I've always figured he's simply too ornery to get sick.

Giving a cat a pill is done in five steps, according to a cat book that I read:

1. Gently apply pressure at the sides of the cat's mouth and cat will open mouth.

2. Insert pill with finger, gently pushing it to the back of the tongue.

3. Retrieve pill from the floor.

4. Wipe blood from bitten finger on your trousers.

5. Try to catch cat and return to step one.

For the past several years, I haven't had to engage in this battle. Lately, though, we've been having a problem with hair balls. All cat people know this term isn't very descriptive. Hair balls aren't round at all; they're just flat, matted glop. All cat people also know that felines never upchuck these disgusting things quietly in their litter box. Oh, no, they find the most sublime places, such as a cherished piece of furniture or your bed (never their bed, you can be sure). A shag rug will also serve in a pinch.

And they are so dramatic about it. They snort, heave, and carry on so loudly you'd think they were bringing up the Titanic.

Spook used to do this a couple of times a year and I managed to live with it. But when this started to become a regular feature of the day, I took him to the vet.

He figured Spook was experiencing some irritation due to the hair ball and gave me a bottle of pills to administer on a daily basis. I was not happy with this news. In fact, I mentioned that I'd rather have a root canal on a daily basis than try to force a pill down a reluctant Spook's throat.

But there have been some medical advancements in this field. The doctor produced what he called a "miracle" device (even veterinarians hate to give pills to cats) that takes the problem out of the ordeal.

He showed me this thing that looks like an oversized syringe. One end has a plunger. The other end, instead of a needle, has a rubber thing into which you insert the pill. Then all you have to do is open the cat's mouth (see step one), push this to the back of his throat, and depress the plunger.

"He can't bite you and has no choice but to swallow the pill," the vet announced happily, showing me how it worked.

Well, happy day! The perfect invention. I couldn't wait to try it out for myself.

Unfortunately what worked to perfection in the vet's office wasn't quite so efficient at home.

Spook, like all cats, knows when he's dealing with an inept amateur. With the vet, he was too smart to protest because he was in unfamiliar territory and he knew the guy was a pro. However, at home, everything changed. He knew who was in charge and immediately let me know what he thought of my "miracle" device. The first try he just slapped it out of my hand with a disdainful hiss.

I tried again with a firmer grip and just when I thought I had everything right, he jerked his head back as I depressed the plunger and the pill bounced off his eye.

This has been the norm. I rarely get a pill actually inside him.

Once I even tried it on myself to show him how harmless it is.

It hasn't made it any more acceptable to Spook.

However, some good has come of it.

I don't have any hair balls.